ROCKS

and What They Tell Us

by Lester del Rey

illustrated by Pru Herric

Prepared under the editorial direction of
Dr. Sturges W. Bailey, Department of Geology,
The University of Wisconsin.

WHITMAN PUBLISHING COMPANY
Racine, Wisconsin

Contents

Library of Congress Catalog Card Number: 61-9975

Printed in the U.S.A.

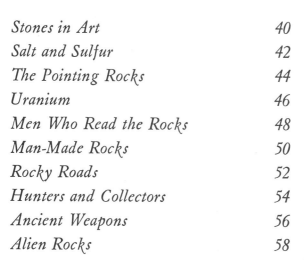

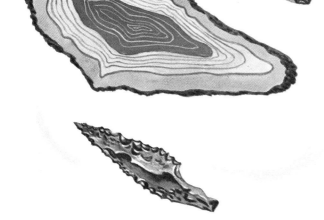

Rocks

ROCKS MAKE UP MOST OF THE EARTH on which we live. The mountains are built of rocks. The plains and oceans rest on deep layers of rocks. Even in outer space, there are rocks circling the sun like tiny planets.

Rocks are also our best record of what happened in the distant past. Weapons of stone show how early man lived. Other rocks have preserved the footprints of dinosaurs and the shape of the earliest life about which we know.

In fact, a great deal of what we know about our world has come to us from a study of rocks.

Rocks That Change

MOST PEOPLE THINK THAT ROCKS NEVER CHANGE, but this is not true. Most rocks are constantly changing in size, shape, and even in their inner nature. The changes take place very slowly.

Through a microscope, tiny cracks can be seen in most rocks. Large rocks often break along cracks like these, producing smaller rocks. Wind and weather slowly wear away the largest stones. Water from rain, snow, or the action of streams erodes them. In time, larger rocks become smaller and smaller. At last nothing is left of them but fine grains of sand and clay. This fine rock becomes our soil.

Rains, floods, and rivers wash the soil down to the sea, where it settles to the bottom. Sand and clay—often mixed with other things to make what we call mud—settle in deep layers on the ocean floor.

Waves, wind, and rain wear away rock.

a

b

c

d

This cross section shows how lime deposits have become cemented together to form limestone.

At the bottom of such layers, called *deposits,* the pressure often becomes very great. The fine grains of material are forced together so tightly that they become solid rock again. Sometimes minerals dissolved in the water, such as lime, combine with the material at the bottom, to act as a cement. Rock which was worn away to soil becomes rock again.

High mountains of hundreds of millions of years ago were worn away to become the gently rolling hills of today.

The surface of the earth also changes. The hills and mountains gradually wear away as their rocks are broken up to form soil. This soil is carried away by water to fill the lower valleys, until hills and valleys are almost level.

Other changes occur, also. Great forces inside the earth which are still not well understood lift new chains of mountains. Sometimes these mountains are raised from the bottom of a sea, like the volcanic mountains we find in the Pacific today. To balance these new mountains, other parts of the earth's crust sometimes sink, to fill with water and become new seas. Many scientists think that the Mediterranean Ocean is such a sea.

Mountains exist under the seas, too. Some are higher than any found on land.

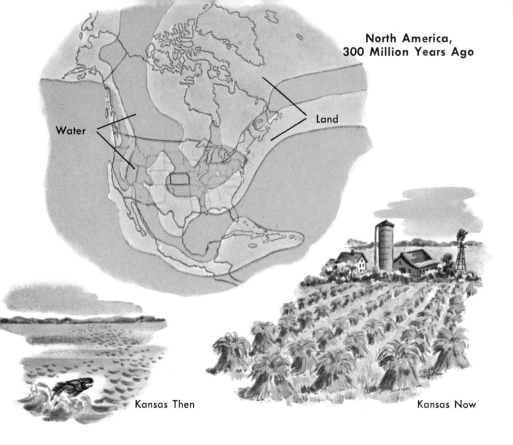

North America,
300 Million Years Ago

Water

Land

Kansas Then

Kansas Now

Three hundred million years ago there was an ocean where the Rocky Mountains are today, while much of the North Atlantic was dry land.

This changing of the surface of the earth brings the sea-made rock up on land again, where men can study the changes that have taken place. Sometimes the change from dry land to sea and back again has occurred many times in one place. This gives us a record of the past that can be traced back for hundreds of millions of years.

13

The Records of Life

Trilobites

Dalmanite
Selenurus

Phillipsia
Portlocki

HALF A BILLION YEARS AGO, tiny creatures called *trilobites* left their pictures inside the rocks being formed on the sea bottoms. We can still see them as little shells, less than four inches long, where splits in the rock expose them. Such evidence we call *fossils*—the preserved forms of life that lived long ago.

These trilobites were very early ancestors of the lobster. They were the first form of life with well-formed shells. When they died and their soft parts decayed or were eaten, the shells drifted to the bottom. Limy mud settled over the shells or filled up the space where the soft parts had been. As the mud hardened into rock, it kept the shape of the shell. Much later, when the rock cracked, it usually split apart where the shell had been, thus showing us a picture of what life looked like so long ago.

There was other life in those ancient seas. Early snails left shells as fossils. Corals grew in colonies, and their hard outer bodies lasted after they died, to build up great piles, just as they are still building coral islands today. There were no land animals at that time, however.

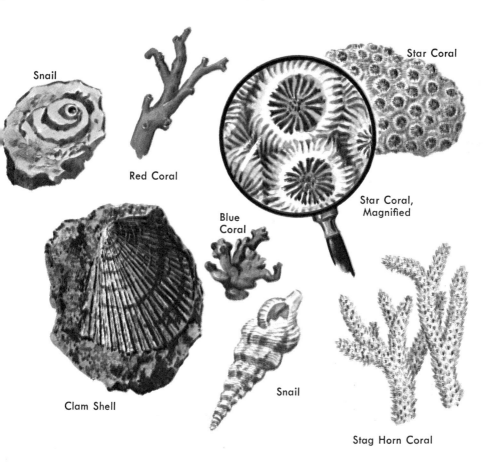

Snail

Red Coral

Star Coral

Blue Coral

Star Coral, Magnified

Clam Shell

Snail

Stag Horn Coral

Probably the first land animals were scorpions, spiders, and later, insects. From these we get another kind of fossil in rock. Insects were trapped in sticky sap from plants, just as they are today. As the sap dried to a kind of resin, it sealed the insects away from the air; without air, there was no chance for decay. In time, some of the resin hardened into a beautiful, clear substance known as *amber*. Inside such amber, we often find perfectly preserved insects from hundreds of millions of years ago.

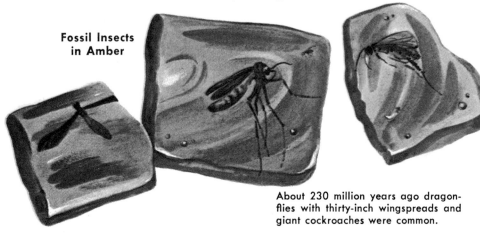

Fossil Insects in Amber

About 230 million years ago dragon-flies with thirty-inch wingspreads and giant cockroaches were common.

One hundred million years after the first trilobites, fish appeared. These were also the first *vertebrates*—animals with backbones instead of external shells. The fossils of such life show us the pattern of the bones, something like shell pattern fossils. Sometimes, however, they became fossilized by *petrifying,* or turning to stone.

When bone petrified, it wasn't just covered by deposits. Instead, when protected from the air, the bony material slowly dissolved, and harder material from the water settled into the exact pattern of the bone.

Fossil Fish

Tyrannosaurus

Most of the so-called dinosaur bones are petrified, and should be called stones. Dinosaur eggs have been turned to solid rock in the same way.

Hen's Egg

A Nest of Dinosaur Eggs

A volcano builds up an enormous cinder cone and buries nearby trees under ash and lava.

Plants can also petrify. There are several famous petrified forests in the United States. Sometime in the past, forests were buried when nearby volcanoes threw out great clouds of ash which settled over the trees, or when the ground sank and they were covered with water and mud. This protected the dead trees from air, and minerals from the ground and water slowly replaced all the cells of the wood. The stone formed in this way shows a perfect pattern of the original wood.

18

Buried trees may petrify. These preserved trees are later are eroded out of the softer rock that surrounds them.

One of the largest of such petrified forests is the Petrified Forest National Monument in Arizona. This covers more than forty square miles. Stone logs lie on the ground and stumps still stand. We can tell that the trees were related to our modern pines and firs. But these petrified forms are at least two hundred million years old. Other such forest-remains in stone can be found which are at least a hundred million years older.

Such petrified trees show the inner structure of the wood, the leaves, and even the seeds. This evidence is invaluable to scientists who try to learn what changes have occurred in plants from the past to the present.

Petrified Cone
With Seeds

Coal

Plants sometimes form fossil rocks by *carbonization* – turning to carbon. The cells of the plants are mostly made of carbon, hydrogen, and oxygen. Heat or pressure can drive off the hydrogen and oxygen to leave only the black carbon. This happens when bread is left too long in a toaster! When wood is covered to prevent decay and put under pressure for a long time, the same process occurs. The carbon produced is called coal.

Three hundred million years ago, conditions were right to create coal deposits in North America. The land was wet and swampy. The climate was tropical. Giant treelike ferns and club mosses grew thickly. As these plants died, their thick trunks fell into the mud. Over millions of years, layer piled on layer, building up pressure at the bottom that was great enough to produce coal.

THIS + HEAT AND PRESSURE = THIS

Coal

The hardening coal preserved the shapes of everything that fell into it. Today, miners find fossils almost every time they dig. The carbonized outer parts of giant dragonflies and cockroaches almost a foot long come to light. Even the bones of fish and lizardlike animals are found. From these, we learn of the coal-forming age of long ago.

Fossil ferns are sometimes found preserved in coal. These trees have been known to have trunks several feet in diameter and thirty-foot leaves.

Stones
From Space

Objects in outer space are called meteoroids. Those which enter our atmosphere are called meteors. Remains of meteors found on earth are called meteorites.

SINCE 1800 SCIENCE HAS KNOWN that outer space is filled with rocky fragments called *meteoroids*. Most are no bigger than bits of dust, but some are huge enough to be called *planetoids*—planetlike objects.

Millions of *meteors* hit the earth's atmosphere daily. Most are so tiny and their speed so great that they burn up from friction of the air. These are the "shooting stars" we see at night.

Sometimes one large enough to reach the surface may

strike. The heat of its fall melts the outside, but the interior is so cold from space that it remains unchanged and we can study what is left. Some *meteorites* are made of iron and nickel. Others are true stones, but the minerals in them seem to have been formed where there was no air. The largest known stony meteorite fell in Arkansas and weighed 750 pounds. A meteorite of iron found in Africa weighed sixty-six tons!

Two huge meteorites fell in Siberia this century. The larger knocked over the trees in a forest and killed animals for miles around in the wind of its fall.

Nobody really knows how these meteorites formed. One theory is that they are the remains of a planet between Mars and Jupiter that broke into pieces.

The magnified polished surface of a meteorite shows the arrangement of the iron-nickel crystals.

The moon is covered with great craters, as even a small telescope will show. Once these were thought to be volcanoes, but most American astronomers today believe they are the result of meteorites which hit the moon. If so, we should find a few "meteor craters" on earth.

Close-Up of
Crater Alphonus

The Moon

Such craters actually do exist. The best known is Meteor Crater in Arizona. This must have been caused by a meteorite of huge size about fifty thousand years ago. The weight of the meteorite has been estimated at 8,500 tons or more. The force of the hit must have been something like the explosion of an atom bomb.

Meteor Crater, Near Canyon Diablo, Arizona

The crater is six hundred feet deep, and it splashes out in a circle four thousand feet in diameter. The outer edge had been pushed up in a ring, like a moon crater, and is covered with nickel-iron fragments from the original meteorite.

Other craters have been found in Canada by photographing the ground from the air. One of these is six miles in diameter. The Canadian craters are all quite old and have lost most of their original look. But they show that earth, like the moon, may once have been pitted with craters.

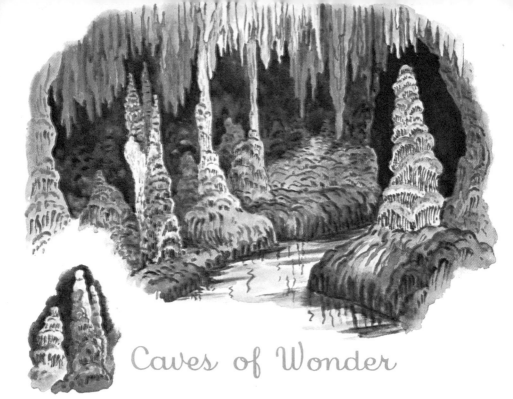

Caves of Wonder

CAVES SHOW US how water can carry away rocks. Many caves were carved by underground rivers. Some were pounded out of cliffs by seas that vanished long ago. Others were made by rain water seeping through the earth.

Water dissolves tiny amounts of some rock, such as limestone. When water evaporates in a pan, the scale left behind is just such dissolved rock material. This action is very slow, but over long periods of time it can carry away great amounts of rock. Mammoth Caverns in Kentucky are so huge that they have never been completely explored.

Many caverns, such as Carlsbad Caverns in New Mexico

26

and Luray Caverns in Virginia, are like beautiful cathedrals filled with amazing pillars. These pillars are rocky formations that grow from lime carried down in water from above. As the water evaporates in the air of the cavern, lime deposits on the ceiling form *stalactites,* like icicles of stone. Where water drips to the floor, *stalagmites* build upwards. When stalactite and stalagmite grow together, a pillar is formed.

Some caves are so old that strange species of life have developed inside them. There are blind, colorless fish, insects, and small animals which are found nowhere else.

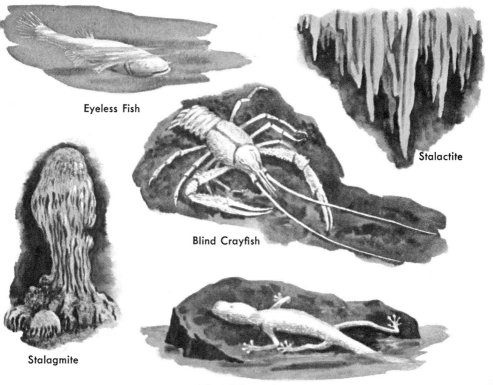

Eyeless Fish

Stalactite

Blind Crayfish

Stalagmite

Blind Salamander

Different Rocks

THERE IS NO WAY OF TELLING how many kinds of rock exist. The same type of rock may even differ from place to place. Without much trouble a trained student of rocks can tell whether a piece of sandstone came from Missouri or New Jersey.

Long ago, however, the rocks were divided into three major classes, sorted out according to how scientists thought they had been formed.

The first class was believed to be the original type of rock from which all others were formed. This class is made up of *igneous rocks*—rocks formed by fire. Such rock is produced by the hot lava of volcanoes or thrust up from the hot inner layers of earth.

Basalt is a basic form of such rock. This is a very heavy, strong rock, varying in color from dark green to almost black. It is found under the sea bottoms and seems to form the base for most of earth's crust.

Basalt

Scoria is a kind of slag that forms on top of molten rock. It has many impurities.

Basalt

Scoria

Perhaps the most familiar form of igneous rock is granite, which makes up many of our mountains. This is made of at least two types of minerals. The fact that it is a mixture explains why it has such a speckled appearance when it is polished.

Polished granite used in building-stones, tombstones, and statues consists of interlocking crystals of feldspar, quartz, and mica.

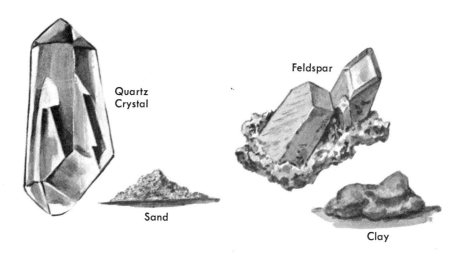

Quartz Crystal

Feldspar

Sand

Clay

One of the minerals in granite is quartz, chemically similar to ordinary glass. The other is feldspar, chemically like a clay. Both quartz and feldspar occur separately, as well as together.

When granite is broken into small pieces, the quartz becomes sand, which is used in making

The potter forms his vase on the spinning potter's wheel.

The glass blower shapes a mass of molten glass by blowing through a tube.

glass. The feldspar becomes clay, out of which bricks, chinaware, and pottery are made.

30

Sedimentary rocks form the second great class. Sediment is material that settles out of water, and these rocks are formed from the broken or dissolved material. As we have already seen, the fine material may eventually be forced together by enormous pressure to form the rocks that tell us the story of ancient times.

Sand becomes sandstone—a coarse, rough rock in which the grains of sand can often be seen plainly. Various minerals in the stone give it different colors, though it often appears red from iron rust.

Clay from feldspar is finer than sand and does not settle out of the water so quickly. It usually mixes with other minerals and organic material found in the sea to form mud. This becomes shale under pressure. It is a fine-grained rock, usually dark in color.

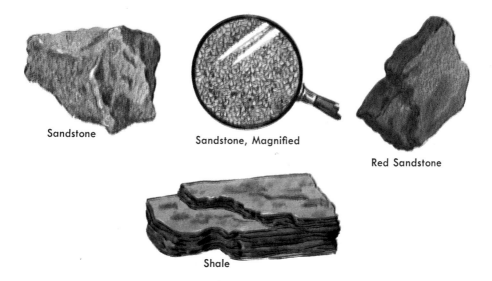

Sandstone

Sandstone, Magnified

Red Sandstone

Shale

Lime settles to the bottom of a teakettle.

Chalk is a soft limestone.

Lime also settles out of water. Rain water contains some of the gas known as carbon dioxide, which is found in the air; water which contains this gas will dissolve lime in much greater quantities than water without carbon dioxide. When conditions change and the gas escapes back into the air, much of this dissolved lime settles to the bottom. Other lime comes from the shells of sea animals. Under pressure, this layer of lime becomes limestone. This is a fine-grained stone that is white when pure.

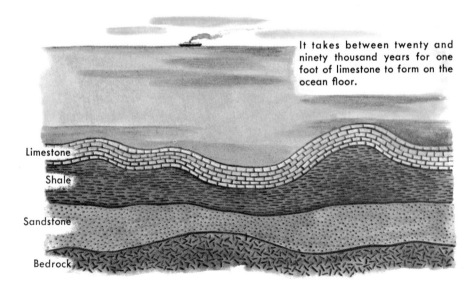

It takes between twenty and ninety thousand years for one foot of limestone to form on the ocean floor.

Limestone

Shale

Sandstone

Bedrock

Rocks may change to a third class, known as *metamorphic rocks,* or rocks that have changed form. Under high pressure or heat conditions over a long period of time, rocks are packed even more tightly together. Sandstone may become quartzite—a rock similar to quartz. Some shale becomes slate. And limestone turns into marble.

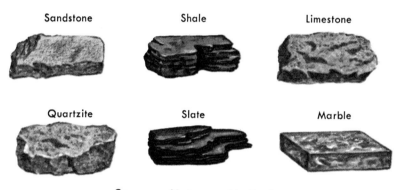

Sandstone   Shale   Limestone

Quartzite   Slate   Marble

Common Metamorphic Rock

During all these changes, many different minerals are mixed together to form rocks different from the simpler ones described here. Others are changed by chemical action. As a result, there are an amazing number of sedimentary and metamorphic rocks.

Schist   Gneiss

Crystals

ALMOST ALL ROCKS are made of crystals. Sometimes the crystals are large enough to be easily seen. In other cases they may be so small that a microscope is needed to look at them. Smooth, worn rocks may require breaking before their crystals can be studied.

These crystals take many shapes. Quartz forms a six-sided rod, and feldspar crystals look like shallow, oblong boxes. Other crystals form cubes, flat sheets, flaky granules, or shapes for which only the men who study crystals have names—such as *dipyramids,* like two pyramids with bases together. When two or more different types of minerals form a single rock, there will be a mixture of differently shaped crystals, and some may be forced

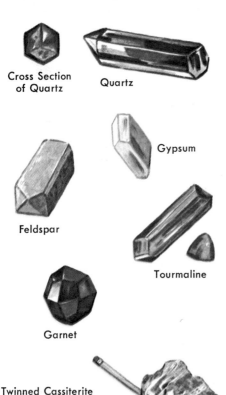

Cross Section of Quartz

Quartz

Gypsum

Feldspar

Tourmaline

Garnet

Twinned Cassiterite

Mica Sheet

Fluorite

Pectolite Needles

out of shape by the pressure of others of a different kind. In rocks of a single material, the crystals may vary in size, but all will be alike in shape.

Crystals in sedimentary rocks are usually small and point in all directions. But under pressure, when such rocks change to metamorphic rocks, the little crystals slide around to point in the same direction and often grow together into larger ones.

Precious Stones

BEAUTIFUL STONES HAVE BEEN USED for jewelry for a great many centuries. The diamond has been made almost a by-word of value. Yet chemically it is only carbon—as is coal. The difference lies in the diamond's crystal make-up, produced somehow deep in the earth under great heat and pressure. Gem diamonds today come mostly from a bluish clay deposit in Africa. Less beautiful diamonds are used for cutting tools, since diamond is the hardest of all natural substances.

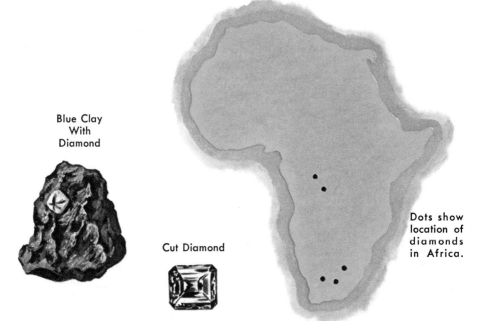

Blue Clay
With
Diamond

Cut Diamond

Dots show location of diamonds in Africa.

Rubies and sapphires are also valuable, but they are made of the same mineral as cheap corundum, which is used for polishing. The value of the gems comes from tiny amounts of impurities which got into them and gave them their beautiful color.

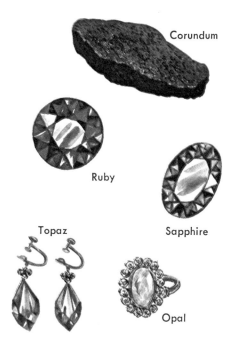
Corundum

Ruby

Sapphire

Topaz

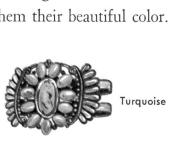
Turquoise

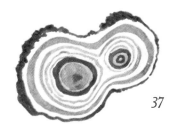
Opal

Many semiprecious stones can be found in the United States. Blue turquoise is found throughout the Southwest and is worked into lovely jewelry by Mexican artists. Topaz of many colors and opals of fair quality can be found in various parts of the country.

Most common of all semiprecious stones is the agate. This is a form of quartz in which traces of impurities add beautiful colors or patterns. Agate can be found in almost every state.

Agates

Uncut Diamond

Cut Diamond

Jewels are more than pretty stones. The real value of both precious and semiprecious jewels comes from the art of cutting and polishing them. Even a diamond does not reach its full value until fifty-eight or more *facets,* or smooth flat surfaces, are cut in just the right way to bring out its fire, or sparkle.

The Egyptians began polishing stones some six thousand years ago. Since only hard stones would hold their polish when worn, such stones were most valuable. But no jewels with facets were made for many centuries. At first, all the artists could do was to cement tough stones to a reed or stick with heavy tar. Then they ground the exposed end into smooth roundness against sandstone or grit—a long and difficult job.

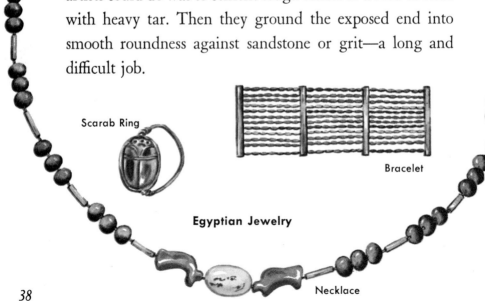

Scarab Ring

Bracelet

Egyptian Jewelry

Necklace

Today, gem grinding is a science. A *lapidary,* or gem grinder, uses a lap wheel of thin copper into which pure diamond dust is pounded. This will cut even diamonds, and the dust from the cutting will work into the wheel to improve it. Small home lap outfits are sold to many hobbyists, who turn out surprisingly beautiful rings, sometimes using only stones they find in their own neighborhood.

Small-Scale Lapidary Equipment for the Hobbyist

Stones in Art

THE OLDEST ART WE KNOW is on the rock walls of caves in France and Spain. There, 25,000 years ago, artists drew wonderfully modern pictures of bison, horses, reindeer, and musk oxen.

Since then, men of all races have used stone in some of their greatest art. The Egyptians used eighty million cubic feet of rock to build the Great Pyramid. Beside it, they carved more rock into the Sphinx, which had the body of a lion and the head of a man.

The Great Pyramid and the Sphinx, built in Egypt about 3000 B.C., still stand after nearly 5000 years.

The Greeks built some of the most beautiful marble temples of all time. They also carved marble into wonderful statues, such as the famous Venus de Milo. In the Middle Ages, many great cathedrals, like the Cathedral of Notre Dame in Paris, were built of stone.

Cathedral of Notre Dame

On Easter Island, in the Pacific Ocean, primitive people carved a large number of stone heads over twenty feet high and left them on the beach. The people are lost now, and we don't know why they performed such a huge task, but the heads still stare out to sea.

Even today, stone is the favorite material for statues and for such beautiful buildings as the Lincoln Memorial in Washington, D.C.

Enormous Stone Heads Found on Easter Island

Salt and Sulfur

SALT, OR SODIUM CHLORIDE, is the only rock which men eat regularly. It is so necessary to the diet that many primitive people travel great distances to get it. The French Revolution, one of history's bloody periods, was partly the result of a tax on salt!

Salt is a true rock which settled out of ancient seas as they dried. Usually, it occurs in the form of rock salt, mixed with impurities. Some of it is mined from deep underground deposits, like coal.

In other places, it occurs as much as 2500 feet below the surface. Shafts are sunk through the rock, and water is pumped down into the salt. This dissolves the salt, forming a brine which can be pumped to the surface. There it evaporates to form our familiar table salt. Sixteen million tons have been "mined" in the United States in one year.

The salt you eat may have been mined underground like this.

Salt Crystals, Enlarged

Another rock, sulfur, is mined in a similar way. Sulfur is a hard, yellow rock which melts at a temperature of about 250° F. Superhot water under pressure is forced into deep sulfur mines, and the liquid sulfur is then pumped to the surface, where it cools and crystallizes.

The huge pumps look almost like oil-drilling rigs.

The Pointing Rocks

WHEN COLUMBUS CROSSED THE ATLANTIC, he was able to steer a straight course because a little piece of rock called *lodestone* pointed in the direction of the North Star. This was a great marvel then.

The first magnetic compass of which we know was used three hundred years before Columbus sailed. It was made of a thin piece of lodestone, fastened to a bit of cork and floated on a small dish of water. Deposits of such lodestone occurred in many places, and the rock was often naturally magnetized by the magnetic field of earth. After its use was discovered, lodestone became very valuable until men found that one piece of it could magnetize many other needles of ordinary iron.

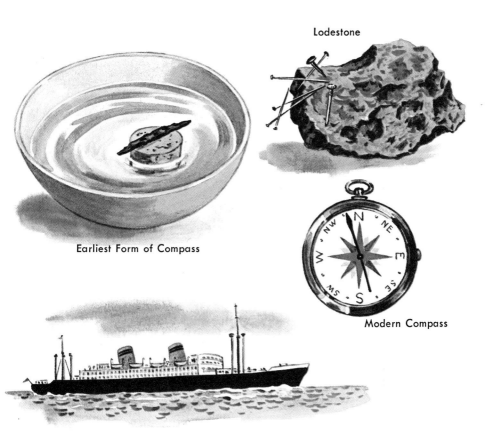

Lodestone

Earliest Form of Compass

Modern Compass

We now know lodestone as magnetite, a black, metallic ore of iron. The black rock is mined for the iron it contains, and over seven million tons are shipped to the iron smelters every year. There giant electromagnets are used to handle the iron that is made from it. Other magnets are used in delicate instruments and huge electric generators.

Even today, however, many ships are steered by the little needle that always points toward the North.

Uranium

IN 1896, A FRENCH SCIENTIST named Henri Becquerel left some rocks on top of photographic film. When he later developed the film, he found that radiation had ruined it. He discovered that radiation which behaved like X rays came from the rock, the result of atoms inside it breaking down. This was the first proof scientists had that atoms could break down radioactively.

The rock, known as pitchblende, was a heavy, somewhat greasy stone of dark color. It was an ore of uranium.

Stoneware Bowl With
Uranium Glaze by Fong
Chow

After that, a little pitchblende was mined for the radium mixed with the uranium. Small amounts were used in making pottery, since uranium compounds added beautiful colors to glass and clay. But there was little other use for it.

One company found ways to purify uranium in the hope it would make better *filaments,* threadlike pieces for electric lamps, than tungsten. But this proved to be a failure.

Then, in 1939, it was learned that uranium was the key to atomic power. After that, more uranium was wanted than the Canadian and African mines could produce. Today, thousands of prospectors listen to their Geiger counters, hoping for the clicking sound that will mean radiation and uranium. The rock that was once useful only to hold down film has become one of our most valuable ores!

Men Who Read the Rocks

MANY DIFFERENT TYPES OF SCIENTISTS spend their lives trying to read the secrets of the rocks. *Geologists,* students of the earth, study the rocks of the seas and mountains to find how the earth is made. *Paleontologists,* students of ancient life, study the rocks for signs of life millions of years ago.

Less is known of the *mineralogists* and *economic geologists* who study the rocks more directly than anyone else. These are the men, however, who are most needed today by our country. They examine samples of ore from all over and report on what valuable minerals such ore contains, and how much. They also make tests by means of small underground explosions, while instruments miles away record the shock wave that travels through the ground. From this record they can often report on what lies far below the surface.

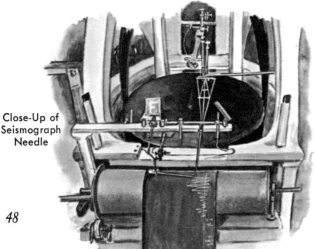

Close-Up of Seismograph Needle

The seismograph's frame and the roll of paper are anchored in bedrock. The needle, or pencil, hangs free. When a quake occurs, the roll of paper moves under the needle and the earthquake is recorded.

48

During the war, Japanese balloons were sent long distances carrying incendiary bombs. Mineralogists examined the sand used for ballast and identified it so well that they could say exactly where in Japan the balloon base must be. Our bombing planes found that the mineralogists were correct and soon put an end to the dangerous base.

Mineralogists identify minerals by means of microscope, X ray, simple chemical tests, and by physical properties such as color, hardness, and crystal form.

Man-Made Rocks

ANCIENT PEOPLE WERE FORCED TO USE, with little change, whatever they found in nature. One exception was clay. Since very early times, men have taken clay, shaped it, and baked it in a fire or an oven. This produced a kind of artificial shale, and some of the pots and vases were very beautiful. Bricks were cruder products of the same method.

Man's second great discovery was the making of glass, perhaps five thousand years ago. This was made by heating sand and a few other minerals until the mixture melted. At first, glass was so valuable that it could only be used by kings.

The Baths
of
Caracalla
in Rome

The Romans invented cement. By baking lime-bearing rocks, they obtained a powder that could be mixed with water to make something like limestone when it hardened. Cement still is extremely important to us.

Today we make a great many rocklike substances. The nose cone of a rocket is made of ceramic—a special heat-resistant kind of pottery. We even make rubies and sapphires. These are ground and polished into bearings for watches and rocket instruments. Millions of such cheap jewels are made because they can be both harder and smoother than the best metal bearings.

Watch Jewels, Greatly Enlarged

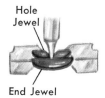

Hole Jewel

End Jewel

Pallet Jewel

Roller Jewel

Rocky Roads

GOOD ROADS HAVE ALWAYS BEEN IMPORTANT. Armies must move quickly, food must be brought from distant places, and messages must be sent reliably. Roads must not freeze in winter or turn to mud in summer.

One of the greatest roads of all time was built high in the Andes Mountains of Peru by primitive Indians. The road, made of stone blocks, runs for thousands of miles through mountains and over canyons and rivers. How these people cut and moved the stone is unknown, but much of the road still stands.

Close-Up of an Inca Road Showing the Drainage System

Road Between Vilcas and Machu Picchu

Ancient China built a road on top of a stone wall meant to keep out invaders. The Great Wall stretched for more than a thousand miles and was so wide that armies could march along its top.

Rome also built excellent roads for her armies to travel. These roads were paved with crushed rock. Some were so well built that they are still being used after two thousand years.

In America, we are building more roads than any other civilization, using great machines to do the work. Crushed rock and gravel are used to form the base. This is then often covered with cement, an artificial stone, as the pavement. It is still almost impossible to build good roads without rocks.

Hunters and Collectors

HUNTING AND COLLECTING ROCKS has become one of the favorite hobbies in America. At least five million people now spend some of their time hunting for interesting rocks for collections or searching for semiprecious stones.

Most of the science magazines carry advertisements for rock collections. Almost every hobby shop has both cheap and very expensive collections for sale.

Such a ready-made collection can be helpful, but it is not necessary. Rocks can be found along every beach and roadway. The collector needs only to know what to seek. For help in this, hobby shops and many bookstores carry excellent books.

The best help will usually come from a science teacher. If the teacher is not interested in rock collecting herself, she can usually tell a beginning collector where to get the information. Also, most local libraries have excellent books and possibly copies of magazines devoted to this new hobby.

The teacher or librarian can no doubt find the address of a nearby club whose members will be glad to help any beginner.

Building a good collection requires study and patient hunting, but it can be the most rewarding hobby possible, as well as one of the most interesting.

Ancient Weapons

LONG BEFORE THE DISCOVERY OF METAL, primitive men had only stones to work with. The first weapon was simply a sharp-edged rock big enough to hold. Then someone discovered how to chip flint. This is a form of quartz with some impurities that give it a grayish or brownish color. A fine flake can be chipped off by pressing sharply with another stone near an edge. With enough such chipping, the stone can be given any shape.

Stone knives for hunting and preparing skins were made then. Heads of spears and excellent stone axes were developed.

Primitive men made weapons of stone.

Primitive women used sharp stone scrapers to clean skins.

Later, about thirty thousand years ago, men learned how to make bows and arrows, with arrowheads of stone. They also began grinding their stone weapons instead of chipping them. When men finally learned to plant and raise grain, they even made sickles and hoes of stone.

No very primitive men existed in North America. But when the Indians came here, they brought a Stone Age culture with them, and stone weapons were used until the white men came. Sometimes an arrowhead or stone tomahawk, very much like those our own ancestors once used in Europe, can still be found around old Indian trails and encampments.

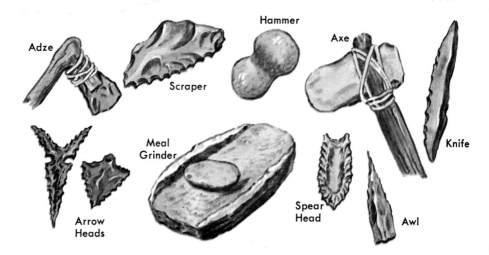

Adze

Scraper

Hammer

Axe

Knife

Meal Grinder

Arrow Heads

Spear Head

Awl

Alien Rocks

SOMEDAY, WHEN MEN LAND ON THE MOON, they will find a whole new world of rocks. Maybe some of the rocks will be volcanic; maybe not. We do not yet know. But many rocks on the moon are surely different from those on earth.

Most of our rocks were formed inside a thick layer of air, and oxygen is one of the chief elements in many rocks. Science believes there is no air on the moon. That must make many of the moon's rocks unlike anything we know.

From the difference, we will learn much more about all rocks—including those we already have.

Who knows what the rocks will be like on the moon, or Mars, or Planetoid X? Perhaps *you* will be able to tell *us* some day!

What is a "GISMO"?

Can you bounce a Ping-pong ball on water?

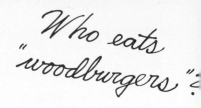
Who eats "woodburgers"?

You'll learn about these interesting things in the

Whitman Learn About Books

Have you often wondered about the trees, flowers, and animals that you see in the park or forest? And wouldn't you like to learn about how planes fly, and why a big building goes way down before it goes up? You'll find out about these things, and many others, in the Whitman Learn About Books listed below.

1. THE AIRPORT, OUR LINK TO THE SKY
Tells about radar, instrument landings, strange cargoes, what airport crews, weathermen, and flight crews do.

2. ANIMALS OF THE FIELD AND FOREST
Tells about small animals—skunks, woodchucks, opossums—and big ones—bears, deer, and moose. These and many more. Their food, homes, and habits.

3. BIRDS AROUND US
Learn about how birds fly, how they migrate, why birds build different kinds of nests, and how they feed and train their babies.

4. FLOWERS AND WHAT THEY ARE
Are you sure you know a flower when you see one? Learn about garden and wild flowers, how some flowers got their names, and how they are used for food and fragrance.

5. TREES AND HOW THEY GROW
The story of trees from seed to seed, how trees feed themselves, how leaves turn color. Find out what trees do for man—and who ate "woodburgers."

6. OUR EARTH, WHAT IT IS
Learn about the inside and outside of the earth, what causes volcanoes and earthquakes, how the oceans and mountains came to be.

7. ROCKS AND WHAT THEY TELL US
Find out how rocks tell the story of the earth, why we find fossils of sea animals on mountaintops, what rock paintings tell us about cave men.

8. RIVERS, WHAT THEY DO
Learn about how rivers form, how they cut through mountains, why early pioneer trails, railroads, and even modern roads follow rivers.

9. PHYSICS, ITS MARVELS AND MYSTERIES
Learn about why planes fly, how we see and hear, how to make electricity. Find out how magnetism works and why you can bounce a Ping-pong ball on water.

10. THE BIG BUILDERS
Learn about the "gismo," why the Mohawk Indians work on tall buildings, how skyscrapers, bridges, and dams are built.

The Whitman Learn About Books have been carefully prepared with the editorial assistance of specialists in many fields.